Anniversary

CAROL SHIELDS is one of Canada's most-acclaimed writers, and is the recipient of the Pulitzer Prize for literature, the National Book Critics Circle Award, and the Governor General's Award for literature. Her eight novels, two collections of short stories, three volumes of poetry, and five plays have been among the world's best-received writing in recent years. Some of Carol's works are set in Winnipeg, where she has lived for nearly two decades, and where she teaches at the University of Manitoba. Her most recent novel is *Larry's Party*.

DAVE WILLIAMSON is the author of three novels, *The Bad Life, Shandy,* and *Running Out*, and several TV plays. His book reviews have been appearing in various newspapers and magazines for twenty years. He is the co-editor (with Mark Vinz) of the anthology *Beyond Borders,* and his most recent book is the collection of short stories titled *Accountable Advances*. A past chair of the Writers' Union of Canada and a past president of the Manitoba Writer's Guild, he is Dean of Business and Applied Arts at Red River Community College in Winnipeg.

Other plays by Carol Shields

Departures and Arrivals
Thirteen Hands
Fashion, Power, Guilt and the Charity of Families
(co-written with Catherine Shields)

Anniversary

A COMEDY BY
CAROL SHIELDS
AND DAVE WILLIAMSON

Blizzard Publishing
Winnipeg • Buffalo

First published 1998 by Blizzard Publishing Inc.
73 Furby Street, Winnipeg, Canada R3C 2A2

Distributed in the United States by General Distribution Services,
85 River Rock Dr., Unit 202, Buffalo, NY 14207-2170.

Cover art by Michael Boss. Cover design by Otium.
Printed in Canada by PrintCrafters.

Blizzard Publishing gratefully acknowledges the support of the
Manitoba Arts Council and the Canada Council to its publishing program.

Cataloguing in Publication Data

Shields, Carol, 1935–

   Anniversary

   A play.
   ISBN 0-921368-81-X (pbk.)

I. Williamson, David, 1934–   II. Title.
PS8587.H46 A85 1998   C812'.54   C98-920073-6
PR9199.3.S514 A85 1998

Acknowledgements

The authors would like to thank the following people for helping them to convert *Anniversary* from a 1980s one-acter to a full-length play for the 1990s: Meredith McGeachie, B. Pat Burns, Linda Williamson, and Paul Cantin.

An earlier version of this play, entitled *Not Another Anniversary*, was first produced by Solar Stage, Toronto, and premièred October 28, 1986, with the following cast:

DIANNE	Marianne McIsaac
TOM	Robbie O'Neill
SHIRLEY	Jennifer Allyson
BEN	Robert Latimer
GARTH	Andrew Lewarne

Directed by Gene Tishauer
Set design by Kathleen Climie
Costume design by Julia Tribe
Lighting design by Lesley Wilkinson
Stage management and sound design by Eric Nickerson

Anniversary, as published in this edition, premièred at the Gas Station Theatre, Winnipeg, on June 13, 1996, with the following cast:

DIANNE	Catherine Roberts
TOM	Jason Broadfoot
SHIRLEY	Sharon Moore
BEN	Dan Weber
GARTH	Devin McCracken

Directed by B. Pat Burns
Assistant Director: Kevin Longfield
Stage Manager: Sue Stone
Design Consultant: Andrea von Wichert
Technical Director: Todd Drader

Playwrights' Note

Anniversary is a fast-paced comedy built on a triple narrative irony. One couple in the play are married and pretending to be close to separation. Another couple, who are separated, are pretending to be married. The third and overriding irony is that the separated couple are still emotionally together, while the married couple have already emotionally separated.

Notwithstanding the comical nature of the piece, a number of serious questions are put before the audience: What does friendship mean and what are its obligations and loyalties? What does marriage involve, and can original marriage vows sustain renegotiation? When is a marriage or a friendship over? What is the nature of pretence and how damaging is it? And, finally, are we all, in some sense, pretenders?

Each of the five characters in this play behaves foolishly at times, but it is not the playwrights' intent to mock them or their enthusiasms. Tom's passion for the environment, Dianne's redemption through crafts and coffee, Ben's and Shirley's confusion over their private/ public lives, Garth's attempt to mask his pain with irony—each of these characters deserves a presence on that narrow and difficult balancing beam of respect and humour.

Anniversary is particularly suitable for summer theatre and for dinner theatre. Its two acts can easily be rearranged into three acts, and a suggestion for this kind of alteration is made in the text.

It is taken for granted that geographical references will be changed to suit particular audiences.

We like to think this play will bring pleasure, laughter, recognition and perhaps even a little reflection.

—Carol Shields and Dave Williamson

Cast

DIANNE HART, about thirty-eight, an intelligent and humorous woman separated from her husband.

TOM HART, about thirty-eight, a mixture of realist and romanticist, somewhat earnest.

GARTH MORTON, about thirty, a friend of Dianne's.

SHIRLEY FORRESTER, in her early forties.

BEN FORRESTER, Shirley's husband, also in his early forties.

Setting

The living room of Dianne Hart's house.
Late afternoon on a Saturday in February.

10

Act One

(At rise, the stage is arranged as a middle-class living/dining room, far from luxurious, but containing a number of smart pieces. An eclectic mix indicates a sure touch. On the left, visible, is a vestibule and the front door. To the right is an archway to a hall and the bedrooms and, beside that, a door to the kitchen. GARTH comes in through the archway on roller-blades. He's wearing a leather jacket, a skull-fitting wool toque, and a too-long scarf. He finds the wrapped bottle of champagne he's hidden earlier, and goes out to the kitchen with it surreptitiously. DIANNE appears, in casual-chic clothes, and begins to straighten the room. She stops in front of the oil painting.)

DIANNE: Garth!

GARTH: *(Appearing from the kitchen.)* Want me to stay? Just say the word and I'll—

DIANNE: Would you give me a hand with this.

GARTH: *(Helping her take the painting down.)* Are you *sure* you don't want me to be here? I could—

DIANNE: Thanks, but the last thing I want is for him to get the impression you're living here.

GARTH: But I ... almost do ... And I'd like—well, you know what I'd like.

DIANNE: I do know, Garth. We made a promise, remember?—that we'd sit down and talk about it tonight.

GARTH: I don't want to rush you.

DIANNE: I know you don't.

GARTH: It's just that—

DIANNE: It's nearly five, Garth. Maybe you'd better go.

11

GARTH: Are you sure?

DIANNE: *Yes.* And would you mind terribly going out the back door? He could be coming up the street right now.

GARTH: You know what I think, Di? I think you're protecting him. He does know I exist.

DIANNE: Look, this whole business is tough enough without having a third party present.

GARTH: I thought maybe I could be in another room, just in case he gets ugly.

DIANNE: *(Smiling.)* Tom? Ugly? He may get maudlin, but he's incapable of ugly. I really think—I think you'd better get going—

GARTH: Right. Good luck and all that. When should I come back?

DIANNE: I don't know. How long do these things take?

GARTH: Why don't I come back in an hour with some take-out? If the scene is getting heavy, well, I'll be here.

DIANNE: You're a dear. Are you okay on those blades?

GARTH: Road's pretty dry since the thaw. What would you like? Pizza? No, how about Chinese—

DIANNE: Surprise me—

(The doorbell rings.)

GARTH: Okay, I'm off. *(Skating toward the kitchen.)* About an hour, then. Back door or front?

DIANNE: Back. No, front—he's got to face up—no, better to use the back door.

GARTH: And tonight we'll talk—

DIANNE: Hurry!

(GARTH exits. The instant he's gone, DIANNE opens the front door.)

Tom. Come in.

TOM: *(Entering.)* Hi.

(He walks around the living room, looking around with a feeling of nostalgia. He's wearing an overcoat and scarf. DIANNE closes the door and comes into the room, regarding him for an instant.)

You took down the picture.

DIANNE: I want you to have it.

TOM: It belongs here.

DIANNE: I think Ben and Shirley would want you to have it.

TOM: My place is too small for a painting that size. I'd hit it every time I took off my coat.

DIANNE: Speaking of taking off your coat ...

TOM: Oh—yes ...

> *(He removes his coat and scarf, and momentarily wonders what to do with them. DIANNE takes them, brushing lint off the coat collar.)*

That was nice.

DIANNE: What?

> *(She hangs up his coat and scarf.)*

TOM: What you did just then. Brushing off my coat collar. That was *nice*. I never used to notice ... when you did ... things like that. I never—

DIANNE: Maybe we'd better get started, Tom. We've got all the books and CDs—

TOM: Where's Tracy? And Troy—where are they?

DIANNE: Both over at Mother's. I thought it would be best if, you know, if they weren't here.

TOM: Won't they be bored? Troy said the last time they were there, your mother tried to read them *Anne of Green Gables* when they wanted their Nintendo.

DIANNE: *Anne of Green Gables* may be just what they need right now.

TOM: You always had a soft spot for Anne. How come you never gave Tom Sawyer a chance?

DIANNE: Tom Sawyer capitulates to society. Anne transforms it.

TOM: Is that what you want to do with your shop?

DIANNE: I just want to—I don't know what I want to do.

TOM: Where's their stuff? This does not look like a place where kids live.

DIANNE: I put everything away. Less confusing—

TOM: What if I took some of their things over to my place, their board games or something, so they'd feel at home when they visit me?

DIANNE: I suppose, but you don't really have room for—

TOM: God, I miss those kids. You wouldn't believe how quiet my place is. I can hear the guy next door brushing his teeth.

DIANNE: *(Smiling.)* Maybe you could get him to floss instead.

TOM: Do they know I'm taking them skating tomorrow?

DIANNE: Of course they do. They're looking forward to it.

TOM: If I can find my skates.

DIANNE: They're probably here. Well. Where do you want to start?

TOM: Do you know what day it is?

DIANNE: Uh—yes, I do.

TOM: Doesn't that strike you as pretty ironic, dividing our so-called assets on our anniversary?

DIANNE: Tom, you picked the day, remember?

TOM: You're so busy all the time. I'm surprised you were able to get away from the shop on a Saturday afternoon.

DIANNE: Mrs. Connor is perfectly capable. Now, shouldn't we start?

TOM: It's crazy.

DIANNE: Crazy?

TOM: That twelve years ago today we walked down that aisle.

DIANNE: Let's begin, okay? Now, I want you to have the Neil Young tapes.

TOM: What do you mean? You love Neil Young.

DIANNE: I'll keep Carly Simon and Roberta Flack—

TOM: Neil Young belongs here. In this room. This is where—

DIANNE: The trouble with Neil Young is—well—I hate to say this, Tom—

TOM: What?

DIANNE: Well, Neil Young—he sort of whines.

TOM: Whines? I never noticed that. I just remember how you and I—

DIANNE: I thought you should have this chair, too.

TOM: I wouldn't say he whines, exactly. Expresses his feelings, his gut feelings, maybe, but I've never heard anyone say he—

DIANNE: *(Wearily.)* Look, Tom, we can't debate every single item. You're taking the chair, all right?

TOM: But the chair and the sofa are a match.

DIANNE: Chairs and sofas don't necessarily have to match anymore.

TOM: Oh?

DIANNE: Individual pieces are what people want now.

TOM: Just like us—we don't match anymore. We're individual pieces. Is that what you're saying?

DIANNE: *(Sighing.)* I thought you liked the chair.

TOM: I do.

DIANNE: Have you bought a new one?

TOM: Want to know what I've got? Come over sometime and have a look. I've got an apple box and a sleeping bag. My place is so empty, even the dripping tap echoes.

DIANNE: You wouldn't be whining, would you?

TOM: Me and ... you-know-who.

DIANNE: Look, I really want you to have your favourite chair.

TOM: I'm not sure it's a good idea. When I sit in the chair, I'll think about the sofa and all the times we used to lie there in the dark and listen to Neil Young ... whining ... while we—

DIANNE: Then *leave* the chair. But I insist you take the ottoman.

TOM: Hey, Ben and Shirley gave us that ottoman. On our second wedding anniversary—

DIANNE: That's right, but look, it's falling to pieces. Look.

(She grabs the ottoman, stares at it, and with sudden delibera-tion rips the cover violently.)

TOM: They brought it over as a surprise, remember?

(He too rips a piece off the cover.)

DIANNE: They were always full of surprises. *(He tears a side off the ottoman.)* Impromptu was their middle name.

TOM: Those were the days!

(He tears the other side off.)

DIANNE: Well, those days *(Pulling a leg off viciously.)* are over.

TOM: Old friends, old times. God, I hate to think they've just *(He rips off another leg.)* vanished!

DIANNE: We'll never have *(She pulls off the third leg.)* friends like that again.

TOM: At least we have our memories.

(He gives a karate chop to the remains of the ottoman.)

DIANNE: Here.

(She produces a green garbage bag and they throw the ottoman remains into it.)

TOM: Okay, now what?

DIANNE: Tom, please pick something.

TOM: Okay. I'll take the Tiffany lamp.

DIANNE: Uh—no.

TOM: What do you mean, "no"?

DIANNE: You can't have the Tiffany lamp.

TOM: You told me to pick something.

DIANNE: Anything but the Tiffany lamp. My parents gave us that.

TOM: Okay, okay. Uhh—let's see. Right, I'll take the photo albums.

DIANNE: The albums? But—oh, all right.

TOM: Where are they, the albums—

DIANNE: In the closet, on the shelf over the coats.

(TOM goes to the closet; he reaches up to the shelf.)

TOM: Two—three—four albums—hey, is this what I think it is?

(He pulls down a box and shows it to DIANNE.)

DIANNE: The slides.

TOM: My god, I'd completely forgotten them. Does anyone take slides anymore?

DIANNE: It's all video cameras these days.

TOM: Do you know, they have video cameras the size of your hand these days?

DIANNE: If you like that sort of thing.

TOM: I wish we had the kids on video.

DIANNE: Let's not get into that, okay?

(TOM holds one of the slides up to the light.)

TOM: Let's see—what's this? Where's the projector?

DIANNE: I don't know. Tom, nobody shows slides anymore.

TOM: Hey, it's the Yellowstone trip. What do you know.

DIANNE: *(Looking over his shoulder and squinting at the slide.)* Those crazy bears.

TOM: *(Taking another slide from the box.)* Hey, look, remember that little guy?

DIANNE: As if I could forget. He did somersaults.

(They both laugh.)

TOM: *(Holding up another.)* My god, our wedding.

DIANNE: There we are!

TOM: Look at old Ben!

DIANNE: Where's the one of Shirley in that hilarious dress?

TOM: I don't know, these are out of order ...

DIANNE: The kids were looking at them the other day; they must've—

TOM: Then they must've had the projector.

DIANNE: It can't be far away. I'll find it tomorrow.

TOM: Those kids must really ... run amok now.

DIANNE: Now?

TOM: Now that they don't have a father.

DIANNE: They do have a father. You aren't dead.

TOM: No firm guidance. No regular supervision.

DIANNE: They do have supervision. You know they do.

TOM: You still have that under-employed-jack-of-no-trades baby-sitting for them?

DIANNE: The store's giving him a lot more hours now. And the kids think he's a terrific sitter.

TOM: And you think he's terrific, too, I suppose.

DIANNE: He's company. He's someone to talk to. And he's a good listener. He's interested in how the shop's doing. He asks questions.

TOM: I'll bet.

DIANNE: Tom, this isn't getting us anywhere. Let's get to the important things. Now, if you don't mind, I really want to keep the copper fish poacher.

TOM: Oh, I thought I'd like that.

DIANNE: You don't even like fish.

TOM: I've been trying to add seafood to my diet.

DIANNE: You hate shrimp!

TOM: I hate the fat ones with their eyes on the end of sticks. I've acquired a taste for the little ones.

DIANNE: You don't need a copper poacher for shell shrimp.

TOM: Let's put the poacher aside for now. What about the Nordic Track?

DIANNE: What about it? It's mine. You loathe exercising. You always said body worship was self-indulgent and time-wasting.

TOM: I said that when I lived in a house that I could roam around in. I need the Nordic Track now that I'm in an apartment.

DIANNE: Where would you put it?

TOM: It'll fill up the living room nicely.

DIANNE: I won't even discuss the Nordic Track until we decide on the silverware.

TOM: You take the knives and I'll take the forks.

DIANNE: Let's be sensible.

TOM: If we were sensible, we never would have—

DIANNE: *You* never would have.

TOM: It was only a couple of lousy afternoons! She meant nothing to me, you know that.

DIANNE: Tom, we officially did it three months ago. We signed the paper. There were witnesses.

TOM: We could've worked things out. All the things we used to like to do together—even shopping. How many guys actually enjoy watching their wives try on clothes and going to fetch the right size when—

DIANNE: Come on, Tom, say what we did.

TOM: I don't—

DIANNE: It'll help if you say it. Come on.

TOM: We ...

DIANNE: That's it ...

TOM: We ...

DIANNE: Come on, you're doing fine.

TOM: We sep—

DIANNE: Yes? Yes?

TOM: Sep-ar—

DIANNE: You're almost there!

TOM: —ated.

DIANNE: All together now.

TOM: Sep-ar-a-ted.

DIANNE: That's terrific. Now, doesn't it feel good to—

TOM: No.

DIANNE: There's something about saying it out loud—

TOM: —that makes it—

DIANNE: —suddenly seem—

TOM: —true.

DIANNE: There.

TOM: "There"?

DIANNE: You've taken a big step. You've said it out loud. You've faced up to it. It's going to be easier now to get through all this stuff.

TOM: It's never going to be easy. Every CD is a memory, every coffee mug's a milestone—

DIANNE: Millstone, don't you mean? Ah, Tom, let's forget about dividing the stuff up and get Neighbourhood Services to—

(The telephone rings. They freeze for a moment, looking at the phone and then at each other.)

TOM: Wouldn't you think people would have the decency not to phone when we're ... in the middle of an important ceremony.

DIANNE: We could let it ring.

TOM: It might be your ... under-employed friend.

DIANNE: You take all the ashtrays. No one smokes around here.

TOM: No one smokes at my place.

DIANNE: I thought you might've started again. Now you're on your own—

> *(The phone continues to ring.)*

TOM: You think, just because—hey, it could be your mother, couldn't it? Or Tracy? Or Troy? One of them's fallen down her stairs—

DIANNE: Oh, you're right. *(She lifts the receiver.)* Hello? ... It's who? ... Ben! Ben Forrester—my god, where are you? ... I don't believe it ... And Shirl, too? ... Great! ... Well, thank you ... Twelve years, that's right. Twelve big ones ... Tom? ... No, he—I mean, *yes*, he's here, just a sec.

> *(She puts her hand over the receiver and hands it toward TOM.)*

It's Ben and Shirl! They're in town at the Radisson and they want to come over.

TOM: *(In a loud whisper.)* I can't talk to them now! I—

DIANNE: I've already said you're here. You've *got* to—

TOM: *(Taking the phone.)* Hello? ... Ben, you old reprobate! What a surprise! ... We'd love to see you ... You sure? ... It's just a few minutes away and I'd be glad to ...

> *(DIANNE gestures wildly but he ignores her.)*

Hi, Shirl ... Yes, we'll have the blueberry tea poured ... Oh, port, now, is it? ... Of course ... Right, see you in a few minutes. *(He hangs up, looking pleased.)* They're getting a taxi.

DIANNE: Why didn't you tell them?

TOM: Don't we have any port?

DIANNE: *We* don't have any anything anymore. No joint possessions, that is. *We* aren't together. *We* are sep-ar-a-ted. Oh, Tom, why didn't you tell them?

> *(Pause.)*

TOM: They didn't ask.

DIANNE: But—

TOM: I thought you put it in the Christmas cards. You said you'd—

DIANNE: I never got around to the cards last Christmas.

TOM: Y'know, it was amazing—as soon as I heard their voices, I dropped straight through the time warp, back to the old days when the four of us—

DIANNE: Tom, I relied on you. I handed you the phone so that you'd have a chance to tell them.

TOM: And spoil their surprise?

DIANNE: You know it's going to be that much harder to tell them face to face.

TOM: *(Shaking his head.)* We don't … actually … *have* to tell them.

DIANNE: Tom—

TOM: We used to have the greatest times together, all of us. Remember Whitefish Lake?

DIANNE: I remember.

TOM: And that weekend in Montreal?

DIANNE: Montreal was a disaster.

TOM: Montreal was a challenge, but—

DIANNE: What's it been? Four years since we saw Ben and Shirl?

TOM: Three or four.

DIANNE: Three, four—we've changed. They've probably changed, too. In fact, I'm sure they've changed. For one thing, they're celebrities now.

TOM: So they're celebrities. They're still the same old Ben and Shirley to us. I could tell, just hearing their voices. Ben said when they remembered it was our anniversary, they just had to stop over. They're on a promotional tour, he said—

DIANNE: My god, I don't have a copy of their new book. Do you?

TOM: No, but I could run out and buy one.

DIANNE: There's no time now—

TOM: Why don't we say we lent it to your mother—

DIANNE: Mother would never—what about *your* mother?

TOM: My mother! Look, Dianne, for old time's sake, we can *pretend* we're still together. They'd never believe—

DIANNE: Oh, Tom, face it. Ever since you were elected president of the Endangered Species Society, you've lost—well—you've lost touch with reality. We can't pretend—

TOM: We can *try*. I'd rather do that than hurt them, our oldest friends.

DIANNE: That's one of the things that was wrong with our marriage—the trouble you had facing reality.

TOM: Oh, is that what was wrong? I've spent hours staring at my bare walls wondering—just what—

DIANNE: Our compatibility, yours and mine, went the way of the buffalo and the long-tailed weasel.

TOM: Actually, there's still very real hope for the weasel—at the moment, it's merely threatened.

DIANNE: This is getting us nowhere.

TOM: So do we bop Ben and Shirl over the head with the truth as soon as they walk in or do we have one last mellow evening for old time's sake?

DIANNE: I don't know about you, Tom, but I plan to greet them at the door with a résumé of the facts. We might even ask them to referee while we sort through the silver.

TOM: Hang on a minute. I just had a thought. What if Ben's developed a heart condition? Finding out we're sep—might just trigger an attack. Could we live with that?

DIANNE: I think we'd all feel a lot better.

TOM: And what about the Friendship Fund?

DIANNE: Oh! I'd forgotten about that—

TOM: Twelve years ago, wasn't it? All eight of us put in a thousand bucks each—

DIANNE: And there wasn't one of us who could afford it then.

TOM: But we invested in the name of what we all meant to each other. The good old Crazy Eights. We were going to get together and go on the cruise to end all cruises.

DIANNE: In 1998! We signed that ridiculous document—

TOM: Whoever loses touch or gets divorced forfeits their share.

DIANNE: Well, Gordie and Lou are divorced. Are they ever divorced!

TOM: And Genevieve left Whitney and ran off with her—was he her tennis coach?

DIANNE: Her personal trainer.

TOM: So it's come down to you and me and Shirley and Ben—

DIANNE: You're the official treasurer, so you can just hand the cheque over to them—tonight's the ideal occasion—

TOM: We—you and I—aren't divorced exactly.

DIANNE: A technicality. *They* are still together, *they* aren't separated, ipso facto *they* get the money. Why not give it to them tonight?

TOM: One small problem. I don't have the money.

DIANNE: What?

TOM: Part of what I loaned you to set up the shop came out—

DIANNE: —out of the Friendship Fund!

TOM: I'm afraid so.

DIANNE: Tom, that's dishonest! Why didn't you tell me at the time?

TOM: I didn't—I couldn't. You wanted it so much, your own business. You said this town needed a coffee and crafts shop. And I wanted you to—

DIANNE: To what?

TOM: To have what you wanted. For once.

DIANNE: Oh, Tom—

TOM: And I knew you'd make a success of it.

DIANNE: Really. You really knew that? I didn't know you—

TOM: Are you—I don't want to pry—but are you in a position, *now,* to pay back the loan?

DIANNE: No. Not yet, not quite. Another good month or two—

TOM: So all we need is a little time. We'll explain everything, but, for tonight, why don't we play it by ear.

DIANNE: I guess ... I guess we'll have to. But just for tonight. Good god, I'd better check the drink supply. What did you promise Shirley?

TOM: Port. But I'm sure she'll settle for vodka, or—

(DIANNE leaves the room, taking the garbage bag with her. TOM tries to rehang the picture but it crashes to the floor.)

Damn! *(He calls out.)* Do we have any scotch? Remember Ben and his scotch?

DIANNE: *(Calling from the kitchen.)* I'll check!

TOM: Maybe *I* should check if I'm supposed to be still living here.

(He goes into the kitchen. For a couple of beats, there is no one on stage and no one speaks. Then there is a shriek from each of them offstage.)

DIANNE: *(Off.)* What are you doing in *there*?

TOM: *(Off.)* It's where we used to keep the booze—

DIANNE: *(Off.)* Well, I don't keep it there anymore. Please, if you don't mind, stay out of there.

TOM: *(Off.)* Sorry—

DIANNE: *(Appearing.)* That picture. We've got to hang it back up. Quick.

TOM: *(Appearing.)* I will, I will. You know, I can't get over how few traces of me there are around here.

DIANNE: You're right. We'd better—I think there's an old pair of slippers of yours that we could just sort of drop in some conspicuous place.

TOM: *(Still musing.)* You did a pretty good job of erasing me from the scene.

DIANNE: Tom, do you want to do this, or not?

TOM: *(Snapping out of it.)* My clothes! Won't they notice none of my clothes are here?

DIANNE: We'll keep all the closet doors shut.

TOM: What if Ben wants to see my computer? My latest annual report design?

DIANNE: *(Hurrying to and fro, closing doors.)* We'll keep the den door closed. If he asks, your computer is out being fixed—or you've traded it in for more RAM and you haven't got the new one yet.

TOM: My workbench. Ben'll want to see my workbench.

DIANNE: But you haven't taken that yet. It's still here.

TOM: Right. My briefcase?

DIANNE: Uhh—you left it at the office.

TOM: Good lord, the U-Haul out front! How do we explain that?

DIANNE: I don't know. *I don't know!*

TOM: We'll think of something.

DIANNE: It might be best, the minute they get here, to suggest we go out somewhere for dinner. It's a little early, but—

TOM: Good thinking.

DIANNE: Can we all fit in my Saturn?

TOM: I doubt it. We'll go in my—

DIANNE: U-Haul? We'll take a taxi.

TOM: The slippers! Better get the slippers. Oh, and you were going to show me where the scotch is now.

DIANNE: Oh, yes.

TOM: Do we have single malt?

DIANNE: Do you know what single malt costs?

TOM: It's what Ben prefers.

DIANNE: Let's have a look—

(The bell rings. They freeze.)

Oh my god. I think you should be the one who answers it. I mean, would you? Please?

TOM: Do I look calm?

DIANNE: Mr. Rushmore.

TOM: Let's go together.

DIANNE: I don't know what to say. First, I mean.

TOM: Whatever comes naturally.

DIANNE: Should we go holding hands?

TOM: That sounds good—no, it might be too—try to remember the way it used to be when they dropped over and—

(The doorbell rings again, this time with a shave-and-a-haircut beat.)

DIANNE: Wait, I forget, do we kiss Ben and Shirley? Or not?

TOM: Yes. No. Yes. Oh, hell, here we go.

(He goes to door and makes an elaborate gesture of opening it.)

DIANNE, TOM, BEN, and SHIRLEY: *(Shouting together, overlapping.)* Hello! Hi! How are you guys? Hey, look at you! *(Etc.)*

SHIRLEY: *(Enters, carrying a parcel.)* Where were you two? Up in the old boudoir, I'll bet, while we freeze our derrieres on the doorstep. God damn it, come here, you.

(She grabs TOM and gives him an aggressive kiss.)

BEN: *(Embracing DIANNE and patting her behind.)* How's my favourite little Bimbo? Hey, hey—happy anniversary, for chrissake.

SHIRLEY: *(Still hanging on to TOM.)* You look terrific. You *feel* terrific.

(TOM starts to cough.)

BEN: *(Still holding DIANNE.)* This is the greatest. This is tremendous.

SHIRLEY: Together again, the old gang ... or at least half of the old gang.

BEN: It's so damned good to be here.

(He slaps TOM on the back.)

TOM: It's *(Cough.)* good to see—*(Cough.)*

SHIRLEY: Here, just a little anniversary present.

DIANNE: No! You shouldn't have. *(Unwrapping the gift.)* What can this be? I'll bet—

BEN: Three guesses.

DIANNE: It's ... Tom, it's Ben and Shirley's new book! *Rooftops of the World.* Isn't it ... lovely! And so ... big!

SHIRLEY: The perfect coffee table book—all it needs is legs.

DIANNE: *(Reading.)* "We travel from the glazed blue tiles of Japan to the shimmering red tiles of Spain, to the intricate straw and rope roofs of Peru, arriving finally at the dramatic roofs of Canada's Houses of Parliament, glistening under a patina of softest green." Good, some Canadian content.

TOM: *(Reading.)* "Roofs are human beings' crowning achievement, the means by which they protect themselves from the assaults of sun and rain, snow and hail. Whether it be corrugated tin or polished slate, the roof is a ubiquitous monument to civility, a concrete metaphor for our unique quest for containment ..."

DIANNE: *(Reading.)* "Photographs by Ben Forrester, text by Shirley Forrester." Thank you—it's very ... handsome.

BEN: *(Grimacing.)* Hey, what's the matter around here, did the bartender die?

TOM: Sorry, I was just about to ask you what you wanted to dr—

BEN: Okay, where is it? I get first dibs on the ottoman.

TOM: Let me take your coats—

SHIRLEY: *(Giving her coat to TOM.)* You know what Ben said just before we got here? He said, "After all the travelling we've done these last few weeks, I can't wait to get my feet up on Tom's old ottoman."

BEN: Where is it?

(TOM looks at DIANNE.)

TOM: It's ...

[Suggested break for a three act performance: The cast freezes; lights out. The action resumes with TOM repeating "It's ..."]

DIANNE: Not here. Wouldn't you know it! The ottoman was getting ... pretty tattered, and the green corduroy—

BEN: *(Taking off his coat.)* Wasn't it blue?

(He tosses his coat over Shirley's on TOM's arm.)

TOM: *(Struggling with the coats as if they are a terrible burden.)* Turquoise.

DIANNE: It was getting so worn, it was changing colour, so Tom said—

TOM: —I said, "We should get that ottoman recovered," and Dianne said—

DIANNE: —I said ... I said, "Right you are," but Tom said—

TOM: —I said, "I don't know if I can get along without that great old ottoman for very long—"

DIANNE: Tom likes to come home every night—

TOM: —every night—

DIANNE: —and put his feet up on that good old ottoman, and there he is, the picture of—

TOM: —contentment ...

(TOM finally hangs up the coats.)

DIANNE: And I said, "Well, look, face it, you're just going to have to do without it for a couple of weeks. We'll take it over to United Upholsterers, and—"

BEN: I *love* that ottoman.

SHIRLEY: He really does, you know. Well, you know he *must* love it, to mention the damned thing on the way here—

BEN: Hey, listen. *(He takes TOM and DIANNE by the hand.)* There's nothing like coming through that door and seeing the two of you. You're looking great, Dianne. And Tom here—same old Tom. Don't they look great, Shirl?

SHIRLEY: *(Slipping an arm around TOM's waist.)* And *feel* great.

BEN: And this house. This room. God, even the pictures on the wall—hey! What happened to the picture? You have an earthquake here?

DIANNE: I—Tom—I took it down to dust it. It's amazing how dusty—

SHIRLEY: Wait. Wait a minute. These are your old pals, Ben and Shirl, remember? No need to be embarrassed around us. That painting of Ben's *is* a bit of a relic—

BEN: I don't know about that—it's from my pink and orange period—

SHIRLEY: I can understand why you haven't had it hanging lately. You didn't really have to rush it in here just because we were coming over.

TOM: We were not just putting it up—

BEN: No?

TOM: We were taking it *down*.

DIANNE: Yes—taking it down.

TOM: But not to dust. I've never quite liked it there.

DIANNE: Neither have I. The light—

SHIRLEY: Lighting's everything! Let's see. Ben ...

(*She and BEN hang the picture.*)

No, it doesn't look so bad there.

DIANNE: Maybe you're right—

BEN: I'm flattered that you still have it in a place of honour, I really am—

(*He gives DIANNE an exaggerated kiss on the cheek.*)

SHIRLEY: You know, when I walked in here and saw your stuff all over the room, I thought for an awful minute that you were moving.

DIANNE: Not exactly, but—

SHIRLEY: What a relief. You just about put a half-nelson on my heart, do you know that? Sometimes, when Ben and I are in Venice or Singapore or God knows where, and I'm in some four-star hotel trying to get some sleep, I just shut my eyes and conjure up good old number 182 Eldrich Crescent, Winnipeg, Manitoba, and you two guys ensconced here—

BEN: All this travelling Shirl and I do, I suppose it sounds like a helluva good life, but it gets to you. Airports, hotels, publishers, interviews, talk shows. Moving all the time, and the goddamn technology! Always changing. Do you know this new book of ours is on CD-ROM? Then we hit this city—same old icy winds howling down the same old streets—

TOM: Actually, it's been quite mild—

DIANNE: You should've been here last week—

BEN: And the people always tell you you should've been here last week—I love it! And we come out here—the same old twin dormers and the blue shutters, and we come through that door and Shazam! It's like hopping into a time machine. Jesus, this is a solace to the heart.

SHIRLEY: You know, kids, there's not a lot in my life I'm proud of— I mean, let's face it, people buy our books, but who the hell ever reads them? One thing I'm pretty proud of, though—that's bringing you two together.

BEN: The chemistry was right.

SHIRLEY: The chemistry was perfect.

(A sudden silence falls.)

TOM: Well. We all deserve a drink, don't we?

BEN: *(With a croaky voice.)* Christ, I'm *parched.*

TOM: Port for you, Shirl—

SHIRLEY: What the hell. Make it a martini. We're celebrating here.

TOM: Ben—scotch on the rocks, right?

BEN: Single malt only, please.

TOM: I don't know if we—

DIANNE: We sure do. It's the vermouth for the martini I don't think we—

BEN: Hell, do you think Shirl wants you to ruin the gin?

SHIRLEY: Just an eye-dropper of Ben's scotch will do the trick—

TOM: In the gin?

SHIRLEY: Duh. No, in my eye.

DIANNE: What about you, Tom?

TOM: I'll have a rum.

DIANNE: You? Rum?

TOM: Just testing. I'd like a Caesar—but I'll—

DIANNE: No, you stay right here. I'll do the honours. Make yourself at home—everybody.

(She exits.)

BEN: You know, Tom, that bride of yours looks different, somehow.

TOM: She does?

SHIRLEY: Her hair's shorter, and I think she's put on a pound or two.

BEN: She's definitely changed. *(He snaps his fingers.)* You know what it is? She's got ... sort of an air of confidence. Independence.

TOM: Well, you know, she has her own little business now. She got kind of tired of just being a—a—an unpaid domestic. Her words.

SHIRLEY: What kind of business?

TOM: A little shop.

BEN: When did this happen?

TOM: Oh, about six months or so ago.

BEN: Terrific! Just what Dianne always needed. What kind of—no, let me guess. A bake shop! Specializing in fancy pastries, and you call it, you call it ... "Lady Di's", right?

TOM: Well, no—

BEN: "The Cake Walk"?

TOM: No—

BEN: "Hart's Tarts"?

SHIRLEY: Sounds like a brothel.

TOM: "Crafty Cappuccino."

BEN: What?

TOM: "Crafty Cappuccino." A combination coffee roasting house and craft shop.

BEN: Beautiful!

DIANNE: *(Entering with a tray of drinks.)* I think this should do it.

(She hands the drinks around.)

BEN: Tom's been telling us about your little venture. Congratulations.

DIANNE: Well, thank you—

BEN: Takes a lot of capital, starting a new business.

TOM: Well, Di managed—

DIANNE: I found a good backer.

SHIRLEY: *(Raising her glass.)* Here's to "Looms and Lattes" or whatever you call it—

BEN: And to your anniversary, for Christ's sake.

(They all take good swigs of their drinks.)

Ahhh. Glenmorangie, am I right?

DIANNE: I—I think so.

BEN: You know what goes good with Glenmorangie?

(He reaches into his inside pocket and pulls out a large cigar.)

Especially purchased for this occasion in Monte Cristo's Cigar Lounge in Toronto. Hand-rolled on the thigh of a Cuban virgin ...

TOM: I—I thought you'd given up smoking.

SHIRLEY: He doesn't inhale—or at least that's what he says.

DIANNE: Are you going to light up in here?

BEN: If you don't—

DIANNE: Tom's asthma—

TOM: My—?

BEN: I didn't know—

SHIRLEY: You never used to mind when I was a two-packs-a-day chick.

DIANNE: We were so happy when you quit—for your sake—

BEN: Mind if I—you know—just sort of chew it?

TOM: No, no, Ben, go ahead. Chew away.

SHIRLEY: *(As BEN unwraps the cigar.)* This shop of yours, Di. Is it all dried flowers and doorstops dressed as grandmothers—that sort of thing?

DIANNE: And coffee roasted right on the premises.

BEN: Pretty gutsy, getting a new business on its feet these days.

TOM: I wasn't so sure about it at first. I thought the two of us might team up—

DIANNE: But I didn't think it was a good idea to put all our eggs in one basket—

SHIRLEY: Or all your Christmas decorations on one tree—

BEN: Or all your beans in one roaster—

SHIRLEY: You know, Ben and I've worked together for a long time now, but it's not the best idea. No, I mean it, Ben, let me finish. Professional jealousy and all that. It stings sometimes. Ben's been in a big funk all week because—

BEN: Correction—a small funk. Bloody *Maclean's* thought my photographs—in the new book?—were "a touch baroque." Baroque!

SHIRLEY: They loved my text.

BEN: One chimney angle too many, they said. Bloody ignorant ignoramuses.

SHIRLEY: Take it from old Shirl here. You're smart to keep your careers separate. And I'll bet it keeps the old you-know-what alive in your—

DIANNE: Well—

SHIRLEY: When two people see each other all day, every day, the romance starts to get a *leetle* bit—I'll let you in on a secret.

DIANNE: Tell us.

TOM: What?

SHIRLEY: Well, sometimes, once in a while, Ben and I … dress up—

BEN: Shirl—

SHIRLEY: They'll get a kick out of this.

BEN: For the love of Pete.

SHIRLEY: Sometimes, when things get a little, you know, humdrum, well, Ben and I dress up and pretend we're—

BEN: —other people.

TOM: You do?

DIANNE: Go on.

SHIRLEY: Call it role-playing. I've got this Dolly Parton platinum wig and this clingy red sequined gown that I can hardly walk in, and Ben wears his tux and a bunch of rings and he's the show biz impresario who's taking this flashy new torch singer out on the town.

(She stands and snake-hips across the room.)

BEN: Crazy broad.

SHIRLEY: And hey, this'll knock your eyebrows off—we've got this other routine where Ben gets into his blue tights and—

BEN: Is nothing sacred?

SHIRLEY: And picture this—a red cape, and me in my Lois Lane gear—

BEN: They get the idea, kiddo.

SHIRLEY: No, take it from Auntie Shirl, you're better off, Di, in your knick knack and decaf store and Thomas in his graphics business—

BEN: *(Clearing his throat.)* Still playing bridge?

DIANNE: Well, since Tom became president of the local chapter of the Endangered Species Society, we're both so incredibly busy—

TOM: I'm not that busy.

DIANNE: Four nights a week. You don't call that busy?

TOM: The fact is, we've had some close calls in this province. I guess you've heard about our problems with the burrowing owl—

SHIRLEY: Well, no, I can't say that I—

TOM: The problem is, it burrows, as you'd expect it to, but it burrows down in the ground, going after mice, and the mice are full of potent chemicals and—

BEN: So the mice are dead.

TOM: That's the curious thing. The chemicals don't hurt the mice, only the owls that eat the mice.

SHIRLEY: So, you're saying, one man's poison is—

BEN: —is sauce for the gander. Or something.

TOM: And then there's the piping plover—

DIANNE: Tom, I'm not sure Ben and Shirl want to discuss—

TOM: The problem with the piping plover is habitat. These birds are victims of our changing world. Suddenly there aren't enough nesting places for them.

SHIRLEY: Hey, it's a big country. I'm sure if your piping—?

TOM: Plovers—

SHIRLEY: I'm sure if they really wanted to ... *nest (Rolling her eyes.)* ... well, they'd find a way.

TOM: You'd think so, but nesting isn't that easy for highly specialized species. Conditions have to be just right. They lay their eggs on beaches, you see, so they've got to be out in the open, and yet not *too* out in the open or their predators—

BEN: These seem like pretty damn fussy birds to me. Most of us can't afford to be that choosy, we *nest* where we have to nest—

SHIRLEY: Make the best of things—like, what kind of choice do *we* get anyway? And believe me, there are plenty of predators out there to make things messy. Maybe I should tell you about—

BEN: Skip it, Shirl. Not tonight. We're here to celebrate old times. Wasn't it you, Tom, who got the Crazy Eights going?

TOM: I think it was you and Shirl—

SHIRLEY: That was a damned long time ago.

BEN: You know, Shirl and I've been married so long, we're on our second bottle of Tabasco sauce.

SHIRLEY: Hell of a lot of water under the bridge, all right.

BEN: Speaking of water under the bridge, any of you remember how we spent your first wedding anniversary?

DIANNE: Here we go!

SHIRLEY: Wasn't that the year we went to Whitefish Lake, all eight of us? Thomas here talked Ben and you and me into taking out a canoe when not one of us had a clue—

TOM: *You* talked *us* into it—

SHIRLEY: You came on as if you were the expert! You'd been a counselor at Camp Stevens—

TOM: I had not! I was never—

SHIRLEY: You were the first one in the canoe.

DIANNE: He was in the back—

BEN: —giving directions—

DIANNE: —yelling, "J-stroke, J-stroke!"

TOM: No, I was in the front—

BEN: Yeah, I think you're right. You should've been in the back, but—I was in the back. I was here, right?

(He gets down on the floor to demonstrate.)

DIANNE: *(Also getting down.)* I was here and, Shirl, you were there—

(She indicates the space between herself and BEN.)

SHIRLEY: No, no, I was here, in front of you—

(She gets down.)

DIANNE: Okay—yes. *(Pushing herself back closer to BEN.)* Yes, this is how we were.

SHIRLEY: *(Grabbing TOM's hand and pulling him down.)* You were here, Tomcat, right in front of old pal Shirley.

TOM: Like this?

SHIRLEY: *(Wrapping her legs around TOM.)* Yeah, that's better—

TOM: Hey, this is a boat, not a bobsled.

BEN: So there we were, and someone—was it me or you, Tom?— said, "Look out for the goddamn pier!"

SHIRLEY: It was Di. I remember her yelling like it was yesterday. Only, it was more like "Holy mackerel, what's *that?*"

DIANNE: We were heading straight for that concrete pillar—

SHIRLEY: And we were all paddling like mad and the damned canoe wouldn't—

BEN: And Tom kept yelling "J-stroke!"

TOM: I don't think it was me—

BEN: And o-o-over we went!

(They all tumble onto the floor.)

SHIRLEY: And the water was like ice—

DIANNE: And Shirl, you were hanging onto Tom's jacket and—

TOM: —dragging me down—

SHIRLEY: —screaming like mad and Di was—

DIANNE: —screaming at everybody to hang onto the boat and Ben was—

BEN: —yelling at Tom and Tom was yelling—

TOM: I wasn't yelling. I was under the water.

DIANNE: And I said—

SHIRLEY: You said, "My brand new wrist watch, one day old."

BEN: How did we get out?

DIANNE: Wasn't it—

TOM: Gordie and Lou. In that old rowboat.

SHIRLEY: Gordie and Lou to the rescue! Of course.

DIANNE: They wrapped us in blankets—

BEN: —and gave us some hot drinks and we all got high as kites—

SHIRLEY: I guess you heard about Gordie and Lou.

DIANNE: We heard.

SHIRLEY: He actually married that Cathi. With an "i."

BEN: Genevieve and Whitney, too.

TOM: We know.

BEN: Ran off with her fencing instructor.

SHIRLEY: Those who live by the sword die by the sword, if you know what I mean.

DIANNE: I thought he was her personal trainer—

TOM: Can I get up now?

SHIRLEY: Not till you say the magic words.

TOM: Another martini?

SHIRLEY: Mind-reader.

(She untangles herself and gets up.)

TOM: *(Getting up.)* Another scotch, Ben?

BEN: *(As he and DIANNE get up.)* I won't say no.

DIANNE: *(To TOM.)* You sure you can find—

TOM: Certainly.

(He exits to the kitchen.)

SHIRLEY: I don't want to seem too personal, Di, but what's bugging old John Thomas?

DIANNE: Why, nothing—

BEN: He sort of seems not quite the same somehow.

SHIRLEY: The first thing I thought when I walked in here was, Tom's looking pale.

DIANNE: Pale?

BEN: I wouldn't have said pale, Shirl. I thought he looked a bit flushed.

DIANNE: Flushed?

SHIRLEY: Well, under the flush, he looks … pale. Like he's been under a strain sort-of-thing.

DIANNE: The Endangered Species Society does keep him—right now, he's worried about the small white lady's slipper—

SHIRLEY: Screw the small white lady's slipper! I look into those beautiful brown eyes and I see a man in turmoil.

BEN: If something's bothering Tom, he can tell us. I mean, what are old friends for? *(Silence.)* I think that's a good question. I'm going to try it again. Here goes: What are old friends for? *(Silence.)* Let me ask the wallpaper: What are old friends for?

SHIRLEY: I'm not just some ship passing in the night, for God's sake. Tom and I, we went under the water together, remember? The two of us.

DIANNE: I think ... with the two of you arriving out of the blue like this ... well, he was just *surprised.*

SHIRLEY: Hey, hey, hey, that doesn't sound like the Tom and Di that I used to know. The Tom and Di that I used to know loved surprises.

TOM: *(Entering, holding a champagne bottle aloft.)* Surprise! Look what I found in the fridge. Champagne. Dianne, you actually—

DIANNE: But I didn't—

TOM: *(To DIANNE.)* That was nice. That was very nice. Our anniversary! I can't tell you how nice—I mean, that *says* something.

DIANNE: No, it *doesn't.*

TOM: Just a second—I'll get the drinks.

(He exits, leaving the champagne on the dining-room table.)

SHIRLEY: That was so sweet of you, Di.

DIANNE: I didn't—

BEN: It means a lot to Tom. He's beaming!

TOM: *(Returning with the drinks.)* I never expected—what a surprise!

SHIRLEY: We were just talking about surprises. Remember those last-minute potlucks? Half an hour's notice and Di would have one of her famous pastas whipped up.

BEN: And a bottle of wine and we'd be launched for the night. Good old Crazy Eights. We had some good times.

SHIRLEY: *(After a long pull of her martini.)* Is something bugging you, Tom?

TOM: Not now, that's for sure. I mean, right now, I feel—

BEN: Before, when we first arrived. Shirl noticed something different. You know Shirl, she's got an instinct for these things.

SHIRLEY: A sort of sixth sense. I can sniff things out. Come on, Tom, you can level with us. Did you have something else planned for tonight, you and Di?

DIANNE: No, it isn't that—

BEN: A cozy dinner. Followed by—

TOM: No, nothing like that—

SHIRLEY: Well, what is it, then? Tom, take the four of us. If one of the four notices that another of the four is acting sort of distant or different or ... vulnerable ... in some way, shouldn't the first of the four mention it to the second of the four?

TOM: Well, sure—

SHIRLEY: Then what's bugging you, Tom?

TOM: *(Looking at DIANNE.)* The fact is, there's something I should've told you—

DIANNE: Tom—

TOM: This may not be what you want to hear, but—

SHIRLEY: Spill it all out, kid. We're all friends here, remember?

DIANNE: Tom, you don't have to—

TOM: It's just that—

SHIRLEY: You can do it!

TOM: This may come as something of a surprise ...

SHIRLEY: Yes? Yes?

TOM: Dianne and I ... Dianne and I ...

BEN: *(Jubilant.)* Hey, hey, hey! I think I can guess.

SHIRLEY: Jesus H. Christ, so can I!

BEN: Why didn't you tell us the minute we walked in?

DIANNE: Well, we—

BEN: Didn't I tell you Dianne was looking different? I noticed!

SHIRLEY: A few pounds, I said.

TOM: We never expected it would happen to us. Other people, yes, but we were the last—

DIANNE: We should've told you right away, but—

SHIRLEY: I just hope you'll keep working, Di. It'd be a shame to give that up—

TOM: Wait, what is it we're—

SHIRLEY: Di, lots of women your age—

DIANNE: I know, I'm not that old—

BEN: I say: congratulations!

(BEN shakes TOM's hand.)

TOM: You do?

SHIRLEY: And I say, the more the merrier!

(SHIRLEY kisses DIANNE on the cheek.)

BEN: Let's get that champagne opened and we'll propose a toast to the new little—

(The doorbell rings.)

TOM: I'll get it.

(He goes to the door.)

SHIRLEY: Who could that be? More people to wish you well?

(GARTH enters on roller-blades, carrying a short stack of white take-out boxes.)

GARTH: Hey, gang! Anyone like some sushi?

(End of Act One.)

Act Two

(At rise, the five people are exactly where we left them at the end of Act One. DIANNE, BEN, and SHIRLEY are seated in the living room. TOM has just answered the door and is holding it open. GARTH is inside, holding up the boxes for all to see.)

DIANNE: *(Leaping to her feet.)* Garth! Sushi! What an angel of mercy! We were just saying how famished we are.

TOM: We were?

BEN: *(Rising.)* I don't believe I've—

DIANNE: *(Turning to the others.)* Out of the winter and the night comes our very own rescue dog.

GARTH: Dog?

DIANNE: Ben, Shirley, I'd like you to meet Garth Morton. Garth, this is Ben and Shirley Forrester ... and of course you know Tom.

GARTH: *(Confused but ready to follow DIANNE's lead.)* Hey, Ben!

(He balances the boxes on one arm so that he can shake BEN's hand.)

BEN: Great timing, Garth.

TOM: Yeah, great.

GARTH: Tom. Hey, Shirley!

SHIRLEY: *(Getting up and moving toward GARTH.)* Well, hel-lo, Garth.

(She shakes his hand.)

So, this is the surprise you were saving for Di, Tom.

BEN: I'll bet half an hour from now somebody's going to arrive with a cake.

SHIRLEY: So—you live in the neighbourhood, Garth?

40

GARTH: No, but—

BEN: Great neighbourhood. Quiet. Settled. You involved in the Endangered Species Society?

SHIRLEY: You look like a rare specimen to me—but definitely not a burrowing owl.

GARTH: I'm—

DIANNE: *(Flurried, hostessy, speaking with great deliberation.)* Garth is a friend. Garth, Ben and Shirley introduced Tom and me way back when and today, *which is our wedding anniversary*—bet you didn't know that—they decided to surprise us—

SHIRLEY: Hey, don't forget to tell him I was your matron of honour. Gorgeous wedding, Garth. You should've been there. Of course, you would've been about twelve years old.

DIANNE: Here, let me take those.

(She takes the boxes from GARTH.)

Do you think there's enough?

GARTH: I *didn't* know it was your anniversary—

DIANNE: Well—Tom and I don't make a big thing out of anniversaries ... anymore.

TOM: Oh? I wouldn't say that. *(Holding the bottle of champagne aloft.)* Champagne in the fridge—now that says something. That says a lot.

GARTH: The champagne in the—that's—

DIANNE: Tom, you open the bottle while Shirley and I put out the sushi.

(She moves to the dining table and sets the boxes down.)

I'll get the plates.

(She goes to kitchen and brings them out while SHIRLEY is opening the boxes.)

SHIRLEY: Ahh—let's see ... there's the eel ... oh good, the satanically hot wasabi sauce ... pickled ginger ... nosi maki ... soshimi ... here, Tom, try a California roll.

TOM: *(Working at the cork.)* Uh—no, thanks.

DIANNE: You love fish. Especially the endangered ones.

(TOM pops the cork.)

TOM: Ahhh.

DIANNE: And small shrimp, well-steamed.

(DIANNE hands out glasses and TOM pours as BEN speaks.)

BEN: You know, Garth, I was the best man, so it's only fitting that I propose the toast. Everybody got some poison? A little more there, Tom, boy. Okay. To Dianne and Tom Hart on the occasion of their twelfth wedding anniversary—Shirl, what's the gift for twelve?

SHIRLEY: Silk, isn't it?

BEN: May the future shimmer like a fine silk gown—

SHIRLEY: You're veering toward the baroque again, Ben boy.

BEN: And to our friendship.

SHIRLEY, BEN, TOM, and DIANNE: *(Together.)* To our friendship. *(Etc.)*

SHIRLEY: Garth, you too. Don't be shy.

GARTH: To friendship.

SHIRLEY: To Gordie and Lou—damn them, anyway—

BEN: To Genevieve and Whitney, you scoundrels, wherever the hell you are.

SHIRLEY: And here's to nesting.

BEN: One more toast. And this one, ladies and gentlemen, I mean from the heart. Shirl and I rejoice with you in the good—the *marvelous*—news, and I want to propose a toast—are you ready, everyone—a toast to the new addition.

SHIRLEY: I'll drink to that.

(Puzzled, GARTH drinks along with the others. TOM and DIANNE stand with their glasses untouched, staring.)

GARTH: I think I missed that last bit. The new …?

BEN: Addition.

DIANNE: It's nothing, Garth.

TOM: Private joke.

GARTH: Addition? You mean you're going to go ahead and enlarge the bathroom the way we—

BEN: Not that kind of addition, my friend—

SHIRLEY: Oh God, I hope we haven't boobed. Old blabbergums here.

BEN: How was I supposed to—you said Garth was a friend, so naturally I assumed—

DIANNE: *(Changing the subject.)* I'm starving! *(She puts some sushi on a plate.)* Let's dig in, shall we? Shirl—have this—

SHIRLEY: Wait, Di. Now that the cat's out of the bag, how far along are you?

DIANNE: I—

GARTH: "How far along are you?"

DIANNE: Tom—here, try this—with a little pickled ginger—

GARTH: Dianne, what did Mrs. Forrester mean when she said—

SHIRLEY: Mrs. Forrester? Look, Garth, I'm Shirl to the world so I'm Shirl to you, all right? We were just drinking a toast—and by the way, I could use a top-me-up—a toast to the new little one.

GARTH: The new little one.

TOM: Ben, some more scotch?

BEN: Damn right. Best thing to chase down the champagne.

GARTH: This is an in-joke, right?

DIANNE: *(Desperately.)* Shirl needs another martini, too. And we could use some napkins. Come on, Tom, you and I can—

(DIANNE and TOM exit to kitchen.)

GARTH: I have to sit down.

(He drops into an armchair and lifts his feet as if to put them onto something; he looks around, and then sets his feet on the floor.)

SHIRLEY: They sent it to the upholsterers.

BEN: I loved that ottoman.

GARTH: Me, too. When did they send it?

BEN: Last week, I think Di said.

GARTH: I swear it was here—

SHIRLEY: Don't you ever take those roller-blades off?

GARTH: Sorry—

(He begins to take them off.)

BEN: It's not just the ottoman—I'm pretty crazy about this painting, too.

(He points to the picture.)

SHIRLEY: I'll let you in on another secret, Garth. Ben painted that. We gave it to Tom and Dianne for a wedding present.

GARTH: It's impossible.

BEN: Hey, listen! I used to knock off some not-bad landscapes—

GARTH: I mean, it's impossible that Dianne is pregnant.

(The roller-blades are now off, revealing loud-coloured socks.)

SHIRLEY: The mysteries of human biology do unfold in strange but inevitable ways.

GARTH: She would've told me.

BEN: Forgive me, Garth, but are you a *very* close friend?

GARTH: Very, very.

SHIRLEY: You see, we are very, very, very, *very* close old, old, old friends, so it was only natural that they told us.

BEN: But it took them a while before they worked up to it. We aren't based here anymore so we don't see each other as often as we used to—well, Shirl had to sort of bang Tom on the head and drag it out of him.

SHIRLEY: I could tell the minute I walked in here that something was in the air—I've got these deep intuitions—so I just hammered away. I mean, what the hell are friends for?

BEN: Damned good question.

GARTH: Impossible—

SHIRLEY: Let me level with you, Garth. Are you married?

GARTH: No. I mean, I was once, but—

SHIRLEY: When women reach a certain age and they've had their heir and a spare, they're not exactly jumping for joy when they find out they're going to get into the diaper business again.

BEN: It takes a certain amount of adjustment—

SHIRLEY: —and supportive friends.

BEN: Friends like you, Garth, can really help by showing how pleased they are to hear the good news.

SHIRLEY: Do you have kids? You and your ex?

GARTH: No, we made a decision not to—

BEN: Like Shirl and me here.

SHIRLEY: Well, that decision was made for us—

BEN: More or less. But let's not get into—

SHIRLEY: Just one of the many, *many* adjustments in a long relationship.

> *(DIANNE and TOM come back in carrying drinks and napkins and a tossed salad.)*

> Garth was just telling us about *his* marriage.

DIANNE: Oh?

BEN: How long were you married?

GARTH: Two years. Long enough to—

SHIRLEY: Two years! I'll bet you hardly had time to unpack the china and sort out the socks.

GARTH: Long enough to know we were headed in different directions.

BEN: How so?

GARTH: *(Tearing at a piece of fish.)* She liked polyester sheets and I liked cotton. I liked porridge and she liked muesli. I bought a Jeep and she traded it in on a Volvo.

SHIRLEY: You mean you split up over consumer preferences?

GARTH: We knew our relationship was over. And we had the guts to make a clean break of it.

SHIRLEY: You know who a break-up hurts the most?

TOM and GARTH: *(Coincidentally in unison.)* Who?

SHIRLEY: The couple's friends.

DIANNE: Ben, you haven't had any Shirley. I mean *sushi*.

SHIRLEY: Yep, it's the friends who suffer. Look, suppose Ben and I decided to split up. Admit it—you'd both be heartbroken about it. It wouldn't feel right. We wouldn't be a foursome anymore.

BEN: Just like we're not an eightsome anymore.

> *(Silence.)*

SHIRLEY: Okay, I guess I *do* want an answer. If Ben and I were to call it quits, how much would you, our old friends, mind?

GARTH: I'd say, "Go for it!"

BEN: Would anyone mind if I light up this cigar?

DIANNE: Go ahead. Just go ahead.

(He does.)

SHIRLEY: Every time Ben has to face the truth, he lights up a cigar. It's his way of ... burrowing.

GARTH: Personally, I think marriage can be a form of slavery if you hang in there just because you made a promise in front of a few friends in some frothing adolescent moment—

BEN: I don't think Shirley and I—*(He puffs on his cigar.)*—went into our marriage in a state of frothing—

SHIRLEY: In fact, a bit of froth might've livened things up a bit.

TOM: Hey, wait, you aren't really—

DIANNE: You aren't saying—I mean, this is a hypothetical situation you're setting up here.

SHIRLEY: What if ... what if I were to say that Ben's been offered a teaching job in California—

BEN: A regular salary, not so much running around—

GARTH: I'd say, "Go for it!"

SHIRLEY: And what if I were to say there's a novel in me just crying to be born and the only place it can be properly nurtured is in the B.C. interior—

DIANNE: Shirl, this is crazy. I'm not going to listen to this kind of talk—Ben, tell us she's not serious.

BEN: *(Putting out the cigar rather vigorously.)* Well, now, just a damned minute, here.

TOM: Superman and Lois Lane! Come on, you're still the wild and crazy pair—

BEN: I know, I know—hey, look, sometimes we pretend we're about to split up, that we're headed for separate lives—

SHIRLEY: And the best part of the game is the last part, or at least it used to be. The kiss-and-make-up part. Is anything sweeter than that?

DIANNE: It's all a game, then. You're just—

TOM: Toying with—

GARTH: It doesn't sound like a game to me. It sounds like The End. Full stop. Thirty. Curtain.

DIANNE: Oh, be quiet, Garth.

TOM: No one throws away fourteen years.

BEN: Fifteen and a half.

SHIRLEY: They do, Tom. Oh, they do. And maybe that's where we're at.

DIANNE: Counseling! Have you tried marriage counseling?

TOM: If you make a real effort to stand back and see where you failed—

DIANNE: Sometimes you have to negotiate a new contract because—

TOM: —because people change. Nobody stands still. We *say* things are over—

DIANNE: You know, I never did explain why I got into the coffee and crafts business. As a matter of fact, no one's actually asked me.

BEN: I was just about to ask you that, Di. How did you get into the coffee and crafts business?

DIANNE: Well, I thought to myself, "Something's missing in my life so what should I do?" Then I asked myself, "What are the things I love?" Well, I love coffee, good coffee, the smell of good coffee. And I love to be around things, beautiful things, that people make with their own hands.

SHIRLEY: Pot-holders, pots—

BEN: —those wire candle-holder thingamajigs—

DIANNE: Yes, yes. Some of it's art and some of it isn't, but it's still something people put together carefully. And more and more I've been thinking—I've had a lot of time to think lately—and it seems to me that's what love and friendship are. They're these handmade *things*. It's this *stuff*. You have to pat it into shape, you have to tend to it, pay attention to it. You can have the mass-produced kind, but who wants it?

SHIRLEY: Not me.

DIANNE: Like, maybe you and Ben feel your marriage has turned into a piece of dried wood—

TOM: —but you scratch the surface—

DIANNE: —and you find there's something alive—

TOM: —and breathing inside that you'd almost forgotten.

GARTH: Or you scratch a living relationship and find it's dead inside.

DIANNE: Oh, who asked *you*?

BEN: Know what Shirl did in the cab on the way over here? Rode in the front with the cabby and told him he had a nice meter.

TOM: Well, maybe you have to listen to what the other person is saying—

DIANNE: Just what I was going to say.

TOM: You have to *really* listen, not just to the words. You have to say, "What does this person want?"

DIANNE: People can become more flexible if—

TOM: —if they think it's going to be worth it—

DIANNE: —and quite often it is worth it—

TOM: —if you just hang in there long enough—

GARTH: Speaking from experience, I've never looked back. The way I see it, life's a card game. And you have to do a certain amount of discarding.

DIANNE: *(Raising her voice.)* Two years! Garth, two years is a long weekend!

SHIRLEY: Why are you yelling?

DIANNE: I—I don't know.

BEN: I think I do.

SHIRLEY: Because old friends don't want to be levelled with. They say they do, but they don't. Shake old friends up and they start feeling insecure.

GARTH: True. I mean, suppose the situation were reversed. Suppose—

DIANNE: Garth—

GARTH: Just suppose that Dianne and Tom here—

BEN: Our old friends, the friends of our youth. Garth, do you know what Shirley and I gave each other? What Tom and Di gave each other? Our young hearts. Our young bodies. You can't do that again; you only get to do that once.

GARTH: But what *if* Tom and Dianne split up and you'd just found out about it. As old friends, how would you react?

SHIRLEY: I could handle it. I think. But I'd feel kinda bad about the baby.

DIANNE: For God's sake, there is no—

SHIRLEY: Then I'd probably act like most people. I'd be damned mad at them because we wouldn't be a foursome anymore.

GARTH: Maybe you'd envy them for being able to handle a purely natural development in a mature and honest way.

SHIRLEY: Maybe, but, either way, I'd probably never see them again. Or want to see them.

DIANNE: Oh, Shirl—

SHIRLEY: And given my current shaky circumstances, I might even make a play for Tom. Because I always did—

GARTH: Aha!

BEN: Christ!

SHIRLEY: Oh, you're all getting so bloody uptight! Mind if I help myself to another martini?

DIANNE: I'll get it.

SHIRLEY: Let me.

DIANNE: You'll need the new bottle of gin—down in the cupboard, under the sink.

(SHIRLEY exits.)

Ben, this is just a passing phase of Shirl's, isn't it?

BEN: Sorry, little Bimbo, I'm afraid it's more than that. Forgive us for dumping on your anniversary.

TOM: Maybe—maybe—after a few months apart you'll decide you really—that sometimes happens—

GARTH: I wouldn't give you odds. I've got a theory. When you unravel a sweater, you can't ever knit it together again. All you get is a scarf.

TOM: I'd rather have a scarf than nothing.

DIANNE: *No.* Nobody should settle for a scarf. I mean that, Tom.

TOM: Take the case of the small white lady's slipper—

DIANNE: Tom, is this really the time to—

TOM: There's something frightening about the small white lady's slipper. It's beautiful—that's part of the problem—so people pick it. But once you pick it, it won't seed again in that spot. It doesn't re-establish itself easily like other plants. It's as though it loses a sense of trust—

BEN: What exactly is your point, Tom?

TOM: I ... don't ... know.

(SHIRLEY enters with a green garbage bag, and dumps it upside down on the floor.)

SHIRLEY: Look what I found.

GARTH: Hey, that looks like—

DIANNE: It was falling apart. We're having it renovated—

TOM: In actual fact, the ottoman is no more. It has been ... dispatched.

DIANNE: De-acquisitioned.

TOM: It's toast.

SHIRLEY: Why didn't you tell us?

DIANNE: We didn't want—

TOM: We didn't want to hurt Ben's feelings. We know how much he liked it.

GARTH: It looked okay this morning.

SHIRLEY: Just happened to be skating by this morning, Garth?

DIANNE: How about a singsong? A game of charades? Books. Five words.

BEN: "You Can't Go Home Again."

SHIRLEY: "How Green Is My Valley." *(Sadly.)* "How Green Was My Valley."

TOM: Wait. I think it's time we got a few things out in the air.

GARTH: Now you're talking! One thing I've learned—

DIANNE: One thing! You've only learned *one* thing?

GARTH: I'm just at the beginning of the journey—

SHIRLEY: Journey? Life's a bus stop, not a journey.

GARTH: I do my best thinking on buses. I look around at all those sad faces, those eyes and noses and mouths and teeth, and I ask myself, What do they want?

SHIRLEY: And?

GARTH: They want ... some ... one.

TOM: *(To BEN.)* We're old friends, right?

BEN: Right.

TOM: Well, I'm not sure what old friends are for.

BEN: Exactly the question I was asking earlier, but nobody—

SHIRLEY: Old friends are people you can level with.

BEN: Old friends are an endangered species. Like old marriages.

TOM: There's a difference between endangered and threatened, re-member. Two separate categories.

BEN: You've got to be able to tell an old friend you threw out his favourite piece of furniture.

SHIRLEY: Ben and I tried to share something with you here tonight. We said to each other that our oldest friends had to be the first to know—

DIANNE: But we haven't seen you in—what is it?—four years?

SHIRLEY: There was a time when you would've offered us a bed. We get pretty damn sick of hotels, let me tell you—

TOM: Do you know something? If you're both such good old friends, tell me this: How come neither of you has asked one question about the kids?

SHIRLEY: The kids! How are they—Timmy and that cute little Tory! The little rascals!

BEN: Bless their hearts. *(To SHIRLEY.)* It's Terry and Todd.

DIANNE, TOM and GARTH: *(In unison.)* Tracy and Troy!

SHIRLEY: Well, for crying in the sink, neither of you has asked about my mother.

DIANNE: Your mother! How is she? I always adored your—

SHIRLEY: Dead.

TOM: My god, Shirl, I'm really sorry—you should've let us know.

SHIRLEY: You're probably all sitting here wondering, what did she die of and did she suffer and when was it and—

DIANNE: What did she die of?

TOM: Did she suffer?

GARTH: When was it?

SHIRLEY: *(Weeping.)* Two years ago, in White Rock. She was run down by a truck loaded with dried apricots.

BEN: Take it easy, Shirl. Don't go and get all worked up—

DIANNE: Why didn't you write us, Shirl?

SHIRLEY: When was the last time *you* wrote *us*?

DIANNE: At Christmas, I always try—

BEN: We got your card.

SHIRLEY: A *year ago* last Christmas.

BEN: Was it a year ago?

SHIRLEY: Yup. "Best wishes, Tom and Di." Real newsy.

TOM: Di's been pretty busy with the business. Christmas is a peak time in crafts, you know—

SHIRLEY: Haven't you ever heard of the Internet?

DIANNE: I—we haven't got your e-mail address—

SHIRLEY: You could've faxed us!

DIANNE: Tom told you—we're both busy—

SHIRLEY: You know how busy *we* are, and I mean *busy*-busy, but we always find time to send a proper Christmas message—I believe we sent yours by snail mail.

TOM: A proper Christmas message!

DIANNE: Do you mean that photocopied newsletter? That recital of triumphs and trips—

TOM: "Ben's picked up his third Stanbury Award and—"

DIANNE: "Shirl's latest plaything is silver and scarlet with mag wheels—"

TOM: "Two weeks in Palm Springs—"

DIANNE: "Then off to Mount Fuji in March—"

GARTH: My ex-wife? She sends out six-page, single-spaced type-written Christmas letters—they're a sort of chronicle of all the different places she's been laid in the past year.

SHIRLEY: Clear Lake? Grand Beach? Lac du Bonnet?

GARTH: No, the kitchen table, the hammock, the stairs—

SHIRLEY: A joke, right?

GARTH: No, she—

SHIRLEY: Right?

GARTH: Right.

SHIRLEY: So why d'you want to make a joke out of your own—your own—

GARTH: My own failure? I don't know. You tell me.

BEN: Because you haven't faced up to it yet. That's my guess.

DIANNE: That's not true. Garth told me he's—

SHIRLEY: What does your ex really put in her Christmas letters?

GARTH: She doesn't send Christmas letters. She's not organized enough for Christmas letters. She's a mess since the divorce. So am I. As you may have noticed.

DIANNE: I thought you said you were healing. You told me—

SHIRLEY: You want to put this behind you, Garth. Accept your grief. Heal.

GARTH: You know, I wonder what makes people feel they have the right to counsel others. Does a little light go on, letting you know you're old enough and smart enough now to dispense the soothing syrup of wisdom to those of us who sit at the children's table?

DIANNE: Shirley only meant—

GARTH: Shirley doesn't know one damn thing about my grief.

SHIRLEY: I'd be happy to listen.

GARTH: And I don't want Shirley to know about my grief. My grief belongs to me and my ex. I just met you a few minutes ago, Shirley, and you want my grief. Well, it's *mine*, and it's—it's sacred.

DIANNE: We just thought you'd feel better—

GARTH: I don't tell you everything I feel, Dianne. I can't. And you know something? You haven't really asked. Maybe you've noticed that *I'm* the one who asks *you* questions. You never ask me anything.

DIANNE: You're a great listener, I've told you that—

GARTH: You never ask me about love. Did I love my ex? What is love anyway? What's it for?

BEN: Good question, Garth, good question. I was wondering what friendship was for, but love is even more—uh—

DIANNE: I don't think anyone knows what love is for.

GARTH: It keeps us from crying in the dark, that's what it's for.

SHIRLEY: Two people can cry in the dark—

BEN: They can cry right in each other's goddamn faces—

GARTH: That's what I mean. That's what I'm telling you, but no-one listens to a man on roller-blades.

DIANNE: I didn't know, Garth. I mean, you never expressed—

GARTH: Love. Friendship. It's awful—half the time it's hell—but at the same time it's full of noise, and we need that noise. It keeps us—

TOM: Out of danger.

SHIRLEY: Safe. Or pretending to be safe.

DIANNE: But ... should we go on pretending forever?

BEN: At least we call you guys when we're in town.

DIANNE: And we appreciate it—

BEN: So why didn't you call us last year when you were in Vancouver?

DIANNE: I wasn't—

TOM: How—

SHIRLEY: July, wasn't it? Cy Hendrickson swears he saw you at the airport.

TOM: I was just passing through. Just going to a design conference in San Francisco.

SHIRLEY: And you didn't have a quarter for the phone, right?

BEN: We would've come to the airport to see you.

TOM: You were probably in Singapore.

BEN: Well, if we weren't in Singapore, we would've come out to see you.

SHIRLEY: Anyhoo, we arrive in town and we come over to see you, and what happens? Tom goes into his stranger act, and then we hear about a baby that may or may not be on the way, and then you've got this visiting jock who seems to have moved in—

TOM: My workbench. My lathe. You haven't asked me anything about my lathe.

DIANNE: Tom, you haven't used your lathe in ten years.

SHIRLEY: Then there's *The Edible Woman.*

TOM: What's she got to do with this?

SHIRLEY: Margaret Atwood's *The Edible Woman.*

TOM: I—

SHIRLEY: You borrowed it from me, remember? You were going to return it just as soon as—

TOM: I'll mail it to you. I can't put my hands on it right this minute, but I'll mail it—

BEN: You probably haven't even read our book on fences.

SHIRLEY: *Fences of the World. (Looking around.)* I don't see it anywhere.

DIANNE: I'm sure we had a copy, didn't we, Tom?

TOM: No.

BEN: No?

DIANNE: No, we didn't. Have a copy. No, we never bought a copy.

SHIRLEY: Okay, okay, so you never bought a copy. Is that going to affect our sales figures?

DIANNE: While we're being honest, I have to tell you—

TOM: Don't, Di—

GARTH: Go for it, Dianne!

DIANNE: It's about that cigar. You asked if I minded if you smoked a cigar. *(Shouting.)* I mind! I really mind! And it gives Tom hives.

BEN: Sorry. Well, I don't know if you know this, but I've had a very serious operation. Major surgery.

DIANNE: It was in your newsletter.

TOM: I was out of work for three months last winter when the firm laid off a bunch of us.

SHIRLEY: Tough. I've got fibroids. Ever had fibroids?

GARTH: Coffee, anyone?

SHIRLEY: What?

GARTH: I thought I might make some coffee if you—

SHIRLEY: You certainly do make yourself at home here, don't you?

DIANNE: Garth and I are neighbours in the shopping mall. He works in the sporting goods store next door—

SHIRLEY: And he's also the resident caterer. Tell me, Garth, are you the resident anything else?

BEN: Hey, hey, let's all kiss and make up and stop being so New Age honest—

TOM: It might be more honest to kiss and say "good night."

GARTH: If you really wanted to be honest, you'd explain—

DIANNE: No, we wouldn't, Garth.

TOM: Maybe we should … admit it's over.

GARTH: Go for it, Tom.

DIANNE: Wait a minute. There's always room to, you know—negotiate? Nothing's over.

GARTH: I'm with Tom on this one. Time to admit it's over.

BEN: What's over?

SHIRLEY: I think Tom's trying to say, in his usual convoluted way, that this foursome is over. This friendship.

BEN: Maybe it's over, Tom, but you can't take away our canoeing weekend.

TOM: We'll always have Whitefish Lake, okay, but I don't think it's a crime to admit that we're not the people we were—

DIANNE: I don't want to be the people we were.

TOM: Let's call it a night, folks. Let's call it a day.

(There is a long, long, long silence, penetrated by throat-clearing, body-shifting, etc.)

SHIRLEY: … Maybe I will have a little coffee.

DIANNE: Will you make the coffee … Garth?

GARTH: Is Tom finished? I thought—well, I thought he might want to make clear—

TOM: I'm finished … except to say … there's nothing wrong with acknowledging that something is over. It's just that no one ever wants to say the last rites.

BEN: We tried to tell you that our marriage was over and you couldn't accept it—

TOM: How could we? You and Shirl come here together tonight. In all likelihood, you'll go back to the hotel together. I don't want to be unduly suspicious, but that's pretty perverse behaviour for a couple who've—

DIANNE: Tom's got this sixth sense—

GARTH: Speaking of couples who've—

DIANNE: The coffee!

(Everyone freezes for a moment. GARTH exits.)

SHIRLEY: Here we are, the craziest four in the Crazy Eights. Shit. *(With real sadness.)* To think we invested hard-earned cash in our friendship.

BEN: Jesus, that's right. How's the interest mounting, Bimbo? Bet we've got ourselves a bundle.

DIANNE: Ben, please do me a favour and drop the "Bimbo." When you call me a bimbo, *(Shouting.)* I feel like a bimbo!

BEN: Sorry, little B—sorry, Di.

SHIRLEY: I guess the money is all yours now.

DIANNE: How do you figure—

SHIRLEY: The Crazy Eights are kaput and so are the Forresters, so the money goes to the last intact couple.

TOM: But you and Ben—

SHIRLEY: It's yours, okay? Accept.

TOM: But it isn't ours—

BEN: Look, donate it to the Endangered Species Society, if you like. Seems fitting—somehow.

TOM: But—

SHIRLEY: Listen. While the young stud's out of the room, do you mind telling us what he's *doing* here?

DIANNE: Garth's … been very supportive … while I've been getting the business on its feet. He even does a bit of baby-sitting—

BEN: Do I detect a little menagerie a troys?

SHIRLEY: You know what I think?

BEN: Isn't that what we've been hearing all night—Shirley's chaos theories?

SHIRLEY: I think … Garth is a little more than a friend. Maybe everybody isn't all uptight about our friendship, our imploded friendship—maybe they're just not sure whose baby this is.

DIANNE: Listen to me for a change. There is no baby!

BEN: No baby?

GARTH: *(Entering with mugs, spoons, etc.)* What did she say?

SHIRLEY: She isn't pregnant.

GARTH: Didn't I tell you?

SHIRLEY: How do we know for sure?

DIANNE: Because it's the truth. Someone has to tell the truth.

SHIRLEY: *I've* had enough truth for one night. Some people think truth is the only form of honesty.

GARTH: Huh?

SHIRLEY: In a minute, I might start talking about the time Tom and I—

BEN: *(Getting their coats.)* Come on, Lois Lane, we'll take a rain check on the coffee. Time we left.

TOM: I'll drive you to your hotel. If you don't mind riding in a U-Haul.

DIANNE: Maybe Garth would drive them.

GARTH: Me?

SHIRLEY: A U-Haul?

TOM: It's a long story—

BEN: So—you're a big mover these days. *(He laughs falsely.)*

SHIRLEY: *(Slipping into her coat.)* Get a move on, Superman.

DIANNE: Listen. Let's not let the fact that this friendship is over prevent us from ... keeping in touch. Don't take us off your mailing list.

BEN: See you on the information highway.

TOM: I'd like ... I'd like to give the two of you something. *(He takes down the painting.)* You gave it to us when we were old friends. Now it should be yours.

   (He gives it to BEN.)

BEN: But—oh, hell—thanks. If you're sure.

SHIRLEY: It's been ... rotten.

   (She starts to shake hands with DIANNE, then suddenly embraces her.)

DIANNE: *(Taking BEN into the embrace.)* So long, you old ... darling.

BEN: Take care, my little B—usinesswoman.

TOM: *(Embracing BEN.)* Keep those books rolling off the presses.

BEN: *(Gesturing to an empty spot in the room.)* Our next title: "The Ottoman Empire."

SHIRLEY: *(As the four of them laugh and hug each other.)* Christ, this is getting cozy. Time to go. Come on, lover. You, too, Monsieur Chauffeur.

   (She snake-dances out the door, followed by BEN.)

GARTH: About the U-Haul?

DIANNE: Why don't you keep it tonight?

(TOM gives her the keys and she gives them to GARTH.)

It's been an exhausting evening.

GARTH: But ... we were going to talk—

DIANNE: Tomorrow. I promise.

GARTH: *(Taking in the sight of DIANNE and TOM.)* Okay. Okay, I guess. Tomorrow.

(He puts on his outer garments, realizes he's still shoeless.)

Oh. My roller-blades.

DIANNE: You can't drive the U-Haul in roller-blades.

GARTH: What can I—

(DIANNE rummages in the coat closet and comes up with TOM's slippers.)

DIANNE: These will do.

GARTH: Are you—

(He begins to protest, decides not to, and steps into the slippers.)

Bye, then.

(He exits, and we hear a muffled sound of voices, shrieks of laughter. Brief silence. DIANNE returns to the closet.)

DIANNE: Look what was on the floor under the slippers.

(She picks a box up off the closet floor and takes a slide projector out of it.)

TOM: It's not that late. Still want to sort through some of this stuff?

DIANNE: There's no hurry.

TOM: Mind if I ...?

(He gestures toward the projector.)

DIANNE: No, go ahead.

(She hands it to TOM. He sets up the projector and DIANNE smiles, watching him as she sinks back on the sofa. With the appearance of the first slide on the wall, a Neil Young song quietly begins. Slides show scenes of him then her, then the two of them dancing. TOM manipulates the changes of slide at first.)

He silently asks her to dance as the slides change slowly and automatically. She hesitates, then grins, shakes her head, stands up and moves into his arms as the music comes up and the lights go down.

Curtain.)